VERSAILLES

the story
of the castle
of kings

VERSAILLES

the story of the castle of kings

Text and drawings by
Jean Claude Le Guillou

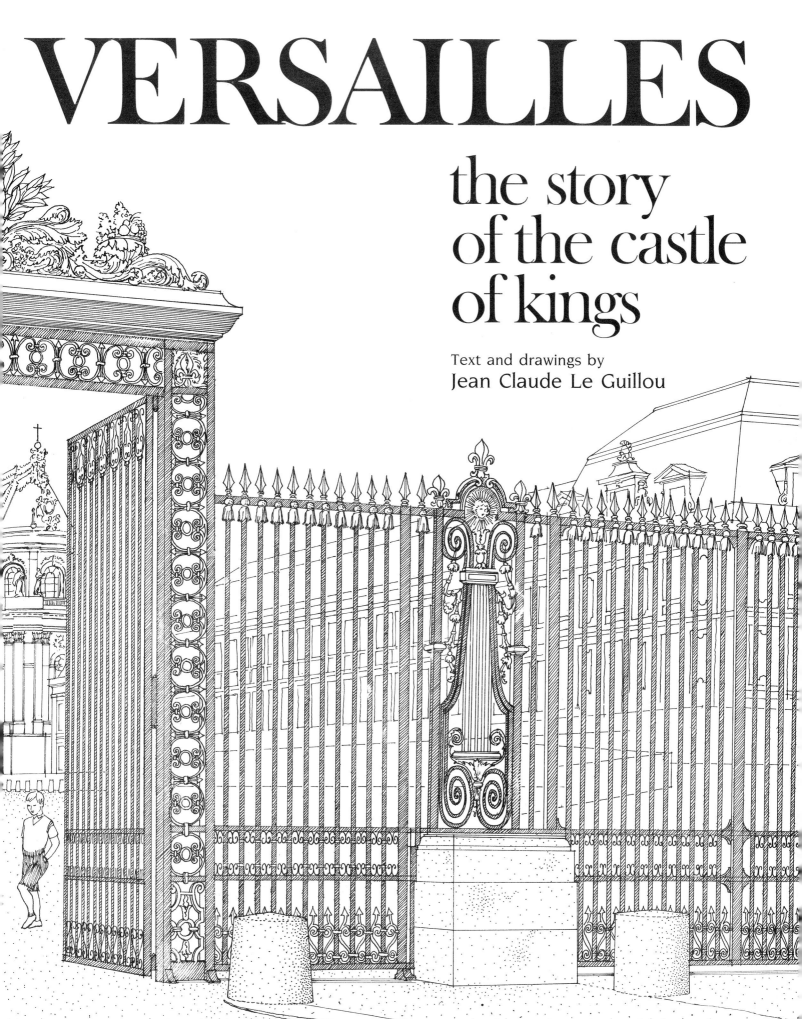

DEUX COQS D'OR

Foreword

The construction of the château of Versailles was a personal affair for the Kings of France.

For a 150 years, they created, enlarged, modified and beautified their residence. They followed the thread of their ideas, the evolution of their taste, their changing needs and the availability of funds.

Thus, they worked in a day to day manner without a unified plan. Their architects were reduced to the simple role of carrying out orders, constructing on demand and without any real opportunity to make decisions.

In these conditions, it was natural that the atmosphere at the Versailles building site was tense.

It is generally unknown, but there was fierce opposition to Louis XIV, the main builder of the château, on the behalf of his hirelings.

Colbert, the Superintendent of the King's buildings, sums up general opinion without mercy : ''The everlasting memory which will remain of the King from this building, will be pitiful. It should be wished that the building will fall down when the King's pleasure is satisfied.''

In recounting the story of Versailles, this book can only side with the King. In it, we will find his own, his father's and his successors' château.

The text and the drawings have no other ambition but to simply retrace the adventure of a house which lived at the rhythm of its owners. This possibly destroys Versailles' prestigious and inaccessible image, but if this allows for a more intimate approach, then we will have achieved our objective.

Translated from the French by Justin McIntyre

This book was edited by Paul de Roujoux, with the assistance of Jimmy Jallot, Jocelyne Galland, Marie-Hélène and Christopher Le Maire.

ISBN 0-7192-1399-1
Original French edition published under the title :
VERSAILLES, HISTOIRE DU CHATEAU DES ROIS
© 1988 by Editions des Deux Coqs d'Or, Paris.
English translation © 1990 by Editions des Deux Coqs d'Or, Paris.

In the year of 1623...

...in September, the story of the château of Versailles began.

Up till then, Versailles was just a large village in the Ile-de-France region. It was situated about twenty kilometres south-west of Paris, on a hillside, at the meeting point of two roads. One, the Paris to Dreux road, went right through the village. The other began at the church and headed towards the Royal château of Saint-Germain, ten kilometres away.

The majority of the inhabitants lived off farming and breeding, but a few of the better off, were innkeepers. The Versailles' inns were very prosperous as the village was on the way of livestock merchants travelling from Normandy to sell their cattle to Parisian butchers. They often stayed the night at Versailles and left early in the morning, herding their cattle the remaining twenty kilometres.

Since time immemorial, the village and the surrounding land were controlled by a squire. In the Middle Ages, the squires lived in a little country manor in the middle of the village near the church. This manor was lived in and looked after regularly until the *seigneurie* * was inherited by the Archbishop of Paris.

This great personage obviously had better things to do than look after his Versailles estate. He let the manor deteriorate, and finally it fell into disrepair. Thus, he had no regrets when someone offered to purchase his *seigneurie*.

The buyer was the King of France, Louis XIII. He was going to build the new château of Versailles and this is a story well worth recounting.

* *seigniory*

5

Louis XIII was a passionate hunter. When he stayed at the château of Saint-Germain, he often went on long forest beats with a few intimate friends. He sometimes strayed as far as Meudon passing through the Marly, Versailles and Porchefontaine woods.

Often when hunting wolves, foxes or deer for an entire day, he sometimes got lost or found himself in the middle of a wood at night.

Exhausted, he didn't attempt to return to Saint-Germain and was quite happy to spend the night in a forest lodge or sleep on some straw in a barn.

Often these long days of hunting finished in the market town of Versailles, at the "Croissant", "la Croix Blanche", "Cygne" or "L'Ecu de France" inns.

These inns were unworthy of a King, but Louis XIII was not unduly worried.

However, his hunting companions were not so keen on this lack of comfort imposed by the King.

These companions, longing for a comfortable bed after a day's hunting, urged the King to build a lodge mid-way between Saint-Germain and Meudon.

Louis XIII approved of their idea and decided that this lodge, or small castle, would be built at Versailles, between the church and the windmill.

As soon as his decision was made, the King gave Jehan de Fourcy, the Superintendent of his buildings, overall responsibility to concerning the construction of the castle.

As the King was unwilling to spend too much, it was decided that the castle would be built with cheap construction materials. The walls would be of roughcast rubble stone and ornemented on the outside by a decor in plaster imitating stone and with a slate-covered roof.

Once the plans and study of the materials were ready, Monsieur de Fourcy had an estimation made of the cost for this modest castle.

The entire project, including plans and quotes, was presented to the King. Louis XIII approved it, but wanted to save even further on the estimated cost.

In order to obtain a discount, it was decided to proceed with a French custom entitled "*une adjudication à la chandelle*". This was a custom which would enable him to rapidly locate the cheapest building contractor in the region.

It was put into practice in the following way:

On the 6th of September 1623, posters were put up in several places in Paris announcing the King's project. The posters described in detail the castle to be built. They also stated that the "*adjudication à la chandelle*" system would be used to choose the stone mason responsible for the construction of the castle. The proceedings were to take place on the 10th of September, at 10 o'clock in the morning, at Monsieur de Fourcy's residence, *rue de Jouy* in Paris.

Six contractors who had read the posters arrived at the rendezvous. Unfortunately, that was five too many, as only one was to be chosen. According to custom, they were all assembled in the presence of the Super intendent and several other representatives of the King, in his Main Hall.

Three candles were placed on the table. An usher advanced to describe the work to be carried out, and finally announced the price which the King was willing to pay for the construction of his castle. He immediately added that the King would be more than happy if one of the contractors could propose a cheaper price.

The first candle was lit. The first contractor to propose a discount was Nicolas Huau, one of the most important stone masons in Paris. His price, however, was too high. Charles Lardier, the second to present himself, further lowered the price. He was followed by Claude Monnard. They carried on bargaining and the candle burnt out. A second candle was lit, then a third. The discussions and bargaining continued.

10

Nicolas Huau had just started to make a better offer when the third candle burnt out. He was thus chosen.

Monsieur de Fourcy was satisfied. He could announce to the King that the price had been nearly halved in the time it took the three candles to burn out.

Nicolas Huau and his builders worked so fast that the castle was finished before the end of the winter.

At the bottom of the court, the main building was erected, it was entitled the *Corps de Logis*. The King's Chambers took up the entire first floor. Underneath them were four bedrooms including those of the captains of the guards. There was also an attic containing five or six bedrooms for the hunters.

The two other buildings, which were called wings, were built slightly lower than the *Corps de Logis*, and were mainly reserved for the servants. The left wing contained public latrines, reserves of furniture and the Chapel. The right wing contained the kitchens and the guardian's quarters.

In June 1624, the digging of the moat, which was to surround the castle, began.

On the 2nd of July, in the presence of the King, the forecourt was traced by marking on the ground the site of the two buildings which remained to be built. These were to serve as stables and accommodation for domestic staff and Musketeers.

The King had slept at the castle for the first time on the 9th of March 1624. As his chambers were still unfurnished, his bed had to be delivered from Paris. In order to gain time and because it amused him, he helped to construct it, in his bedroom.

It took until the end of July for all the furniture to be delivered. On the 2nd of August, delighted to see his castle finally furnished, the King visited it from top to bottom, checking every detail down to kitchen utensils, saucepans and skimming ladles.

At night, he slept fully clothed ready to go hunting at three o'clock in the morning.

Louis XIII grew accustomed to Versailles. Pretty soon, he was visiting it more and more frequently, even when not hunting.

Towards the end of 1629, he installed two *jeux de paume* courts at the castle. This game, very fashionable at the time, is a mixture of pelota and tennis. There were two different types of *jeux de paume*: *longue paume* which was played outside and *courte paume* which was played inside.

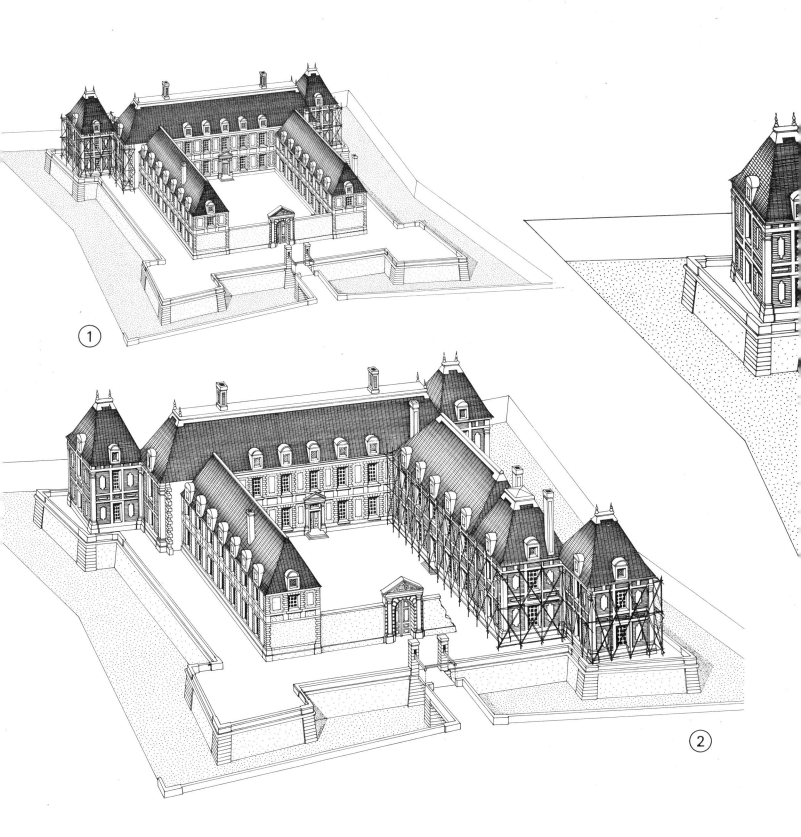

The King was so pleased with Versailles that he soon regretted having built such a small castle and with such modest materials.

In the beginning of 1631, he decided to demolish and replace it with a larger, richer and more beautiful castle. It was to be made with free-stone and brick and would be built on the same spot.

In order to avoid a large building site which would prevent him from staying at Versailles, he conceived a plan to be implemented in stages and staggered over four years.

The construction work was confided to the architect, Philibert le Roy.

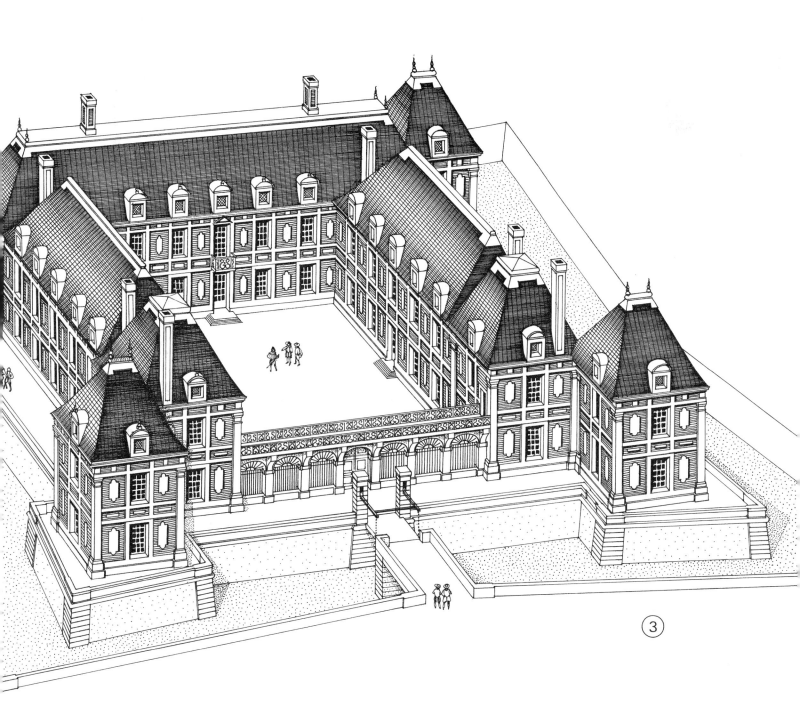

① In 1631, the main *Corps de Logis* was rebuilt. It was extended, broadened and two square towers were added.

② The following year, work was carried out on the right wing.

③ The wall at the bottom of the court as well as the left wing were rebuilt the year after. Finally, in the fourth year, a beautiful arched portico was built to replace the old cloister wall. In 1634, everything was finished.

However, for the Royal residence to be complete,
it needed a garden and a park.

In order to achieve this, Louis XIII had bought all the fields and meadows, portrayed here as they were before the castle was built.

In 1624, he bought the windmill (which he demolished) as well as most of the fields right up to just below the Saint-Germain road (which runs through the middle of the drawing).

In 1632, he purchased the marsh land below the Sainte-Catherine meadow (at the bottom) and a few bordering fields.

All together the estate added up to around 70 hectares, which were to become the garden and the park of the castle.

This is how the park appeared around 1640 :

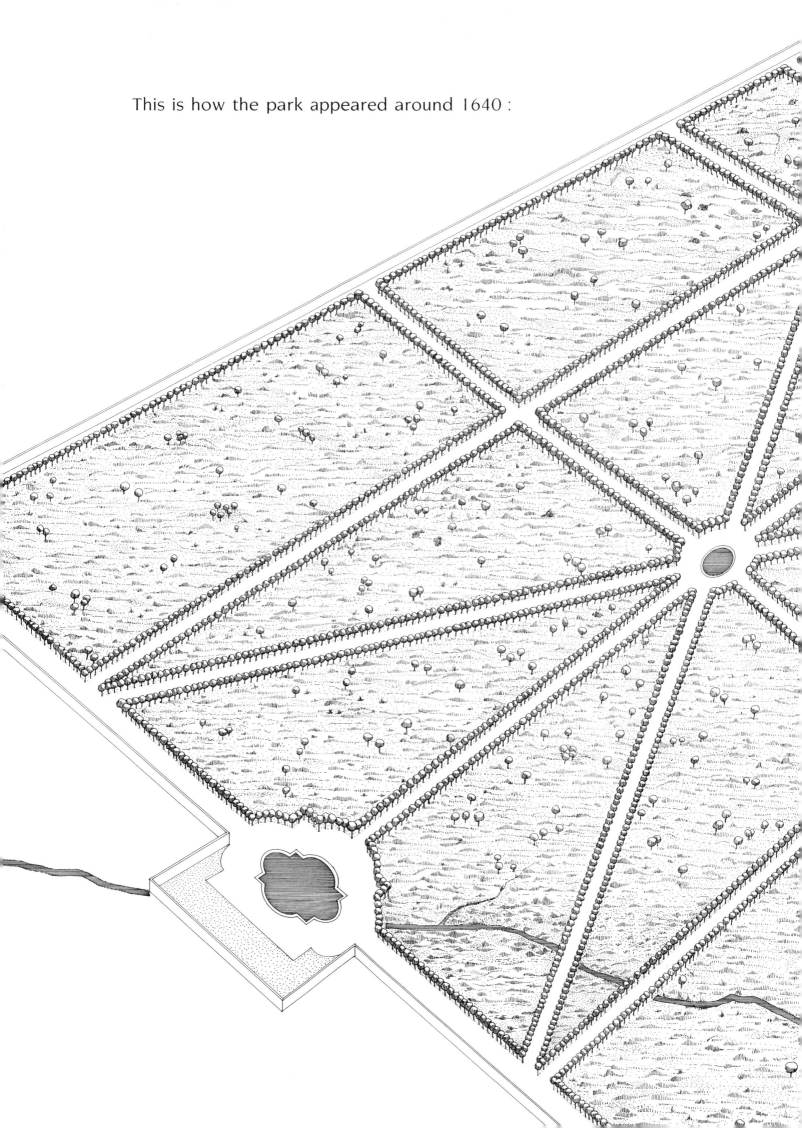

The old Saint-Germain road had disappeared and the old agricultural land was intersected by long paths, planted with trees.

A flower-bed spread out in front of the castle, and a vegetable garden followed by an orchard swept down the slope as far as the main village road.

At the other end, a large basin had been dug to gather water from the neighbouring marsh. Finally, in order to clearly demarcate his estate, the King had it surrounded by a large enclosed wall.

Louis XIII died on the 14th of May 1643, at Saint-Germain.

His son, Louis XIV, did not visit Versailles until a lot later, the 18th of April 1651. He was twelve years old at the time.

He was immediately enchanted. At Versailles, he discovered nature and freedom. He often returned. In the park, he could run, climb trees and hunt. His godfather, Cardinal Mazarin, and his governor, the Duke of Villeroy, were there to look after him and inform him when it was time to enter.

As an adult, he did not forget his childhood playground. In 1660, when he got married and even more so after the birth of his son, he wanted to make Versailles a comfortable country house in which he could come to rest, with his family, from time to time.

As it was, the castle suited him perfectly. The interior had already been renovated several years earlier. There remained little to do before the King could live there with his wife and son, not forgetting his mother, his brother, his sister-in-law and his cousin...

All this amounted to a lot of people. Housing for the servants, vast kitchens and new stables for fifty odd horses had to be built.

Here we see the stables being built, in front of the castle, on the left-hand side of the forecourt.

Opposite, on the right-hand side, kitchens and housing for the servants were being built at the same time.

These constructions were completed in 1663, and in March, the Royal Family could settle down into a completely restored country house.

To further beautify the castle's exterior, the King rectified the shape of the old moats and installed a balcony all along the facades on the first floor. Here, facing the gardens, the balcony passes in front of the King's Chambers, and then in front of the Queen's.

As Versailles was private property, it was forbidden to enter while the King and the Royal Family were there, unless invited.

But the rest of the time, it was enough to demand written authorization to visit Versailles. It was hardly ever refused. It was possible in those days to go everywhere. A valet accompanied visitors, opened doors to all the chambers and gave them any necessary explanations.

After visiting the castle, anyone, if they so desired, could stroll around the gardens and the park until dusk.

After having upgraded the castle, the King concentrated on the gardens.

In 1663, he had them entirely retraced. Only the surrounding wall, the large basin and several paths were kept.

Three grass plots and flower-beds were landscaped around the castle. The southern one, which replaced Louis XIII's vegetable garden, ended with two large flights of stairs which enclosed a building half buried underneath the ground. This building was the Orangery. This is where fragile shrubs, orange trees, lemon trees, etc., were protected during the winter.

The Royal domain had now grown and expanded to five hundred hectares. Louis XIV constructed the Menagerie, one and a half kilometres from the castle on the site of an old farm which he had recently bought. It was a very small castle surrounded by a rare animal reserve.

Several species of exotic birds populated the seven courts arranged around a large dome pavilion.

There was an ostrich court, a pelican court, a beautiful chicken court... A bit further on, were the quadrupedal animals: elephants, dromedaries, etc.

It was not surprising to find a menagerie at Versailles. It had been traditional for the Kings of France, since the Middle Ages, to own an animal garden in the park of their country houses.

Louis XIII himself had already kept a small menagerie at Versailles, where one could admire a multitude of poultry selected for the beauty of their feathers or the rarity of their species.

At the end of four years, Louis XIV felt very proud of all the transformations at Versailles and wanted his Courtiers to admire his creation.

He invited them to a splendid feast which lasted three days and three nights, in May 1664.

But the feast had not been the success the King had hoped for.

On the contrary, despite the beauty of the events, the Courtiers had scorned Versailles, considering it to be a mere country house unworthy of a King. Louis XIV felt gravely humiliated. He did not show it, but he swore that in the future no one would be able to criticize his dear Versailles.

He immediately corrected the castle's imperfections. He increased the gildings and marble, replaced his furniture and finally agreed that his domain should resemble a castle of fairy tales.

His advisors conceived to make it the "Sun Palace". At Versailles, Louis XIV would thus become the "Sun King". In other words a Sovereign, a Star and a God.

The gardens were once again renewed. Fountains and statues were erected everywhere to illustrate the story of Apollo, the ancient Greek god of the Sun.

A specialist of fairy tales, Charles Perrault (the famous author of Cinderella, Puss'n'Boots, Little Red Riding Hood...), had the idea of the Grotto, which is represented on this page. It was an evocation of the sea grotto where, according to Greek legend, the Sun rested at night after falling into the sea. This artificial grotto, built next to the castle, was a sort of enchanted palace entirely covered by multicoloured shells, coral, pebbles and mirrors. Sometimes a multitude of fountains and an organ animated the grotto, as if by magic.

We can see the exterior appearance of the Grotto on page 48, it is the square pavilion with three arches, to the left of the castle.

Nevertheless, Louis XIV did not want Versailles, which was now the "Sun Palace and Gardens", to be too majestic. He particularly wanted his visitors and guests to entertain themselves. He thus adorned his park with strange attractions.

For example, on the hillside near the Menagerie, he installed the *Ramasse*. It was a type of roller coster equipped with a chariot on rails, which hurtled down a breathtaking slope, reached the bottom of a small valley and then climbed back up to the arrival station. Elsewhere, there were swings...

Near the castle, was the Labyrinth which we can see here. It was a small, very dense wood, whose trees had been trimmed to reproduce walls of greenery. The Labyrinth had one entry and two exits. It was intersected into an infinite number of small paths which were arranged in such a complicated manner that one always got lost and had a long walk before finding an exit.

To make it more amusing, thirty-nine small basins were added a little later on, at each intersection. Each basin was embellished with sculptures representing famous fables.

This was yet another idea from Charles Perrault, who had probably been influenced by the fables which had recently been published by Jean de la Fontaine.

With the Menagerie, the Grotto, the *Ramasse*, the swings, the Labyrinth and several other curiosities of this kind, Louis XIV was turning Versailles into an attraction park with which he could be sure of seducing his Courtiers and the general public.

...But the castle itself
remained relatively small...

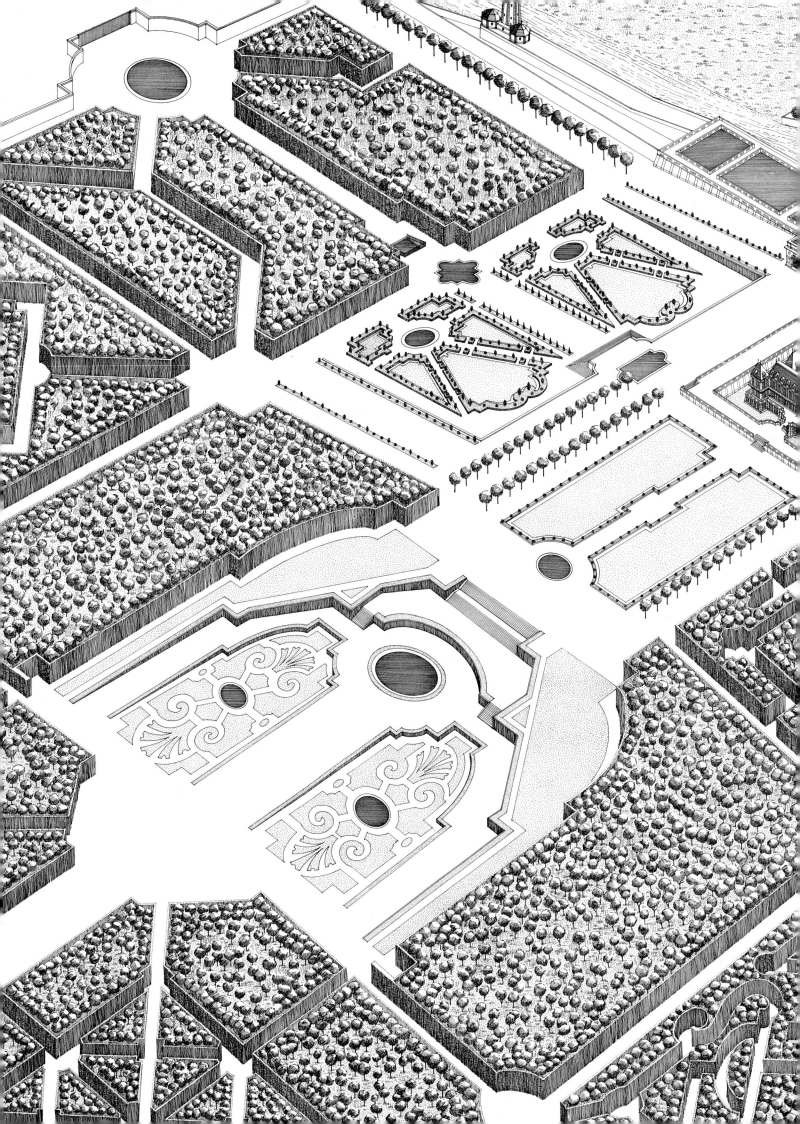

...It appeared to be tiny and lost in the middle of the immense open spaces which surrounded it (squares, courts and flower-beds).

...Around 1668, Louis XIV considered that it was necessary to expand.

For him, this did not pose any problems. In his opinion, it was sufficient to build large buildings around the castle, on the site of the terraces alongside the moat.

Thus, on the garden side, the small brick castle would no longer be visible, as it would disappear behind the large modern and majestic stone facades.

Opposite, on the courtyard side, it would be the contrary as the old castle would hide the new one.

But, Louis Le Vau, the King's Architect, and Colbert, the Building Superintendent, did not share Louis XIV's opinion. The idea of a castle with two different faces (one in brick with slate roofs on the courtyard side and the other in stone with flat roofs on the garden side) seemed, to them, extremely bad taste. They considered the King's project as no more than mediocre repair work.

According to them, as the immense size of the flower-beds required a large building, the only solution was to demolish the old castle of Louis XIII, and replace it with a new, larger and more majestic stone edifice.

The King refused their idea. He was attached to his small castle, and besides he had his own idea of Versailles. He preferred fantasy to majesty, and even if he was the only one to understand it, he believed that the mixture of old and new facades would be more original and gayer than what was being proposed.

The Architect and the Superintendent reluctantly obeyed. During the summer of 1668, Le Vau presented a project which conformed to the King's wish.

The project was immediately accepted.

Work began in autumn.
Labourers filled in the moats and dug the foundations.

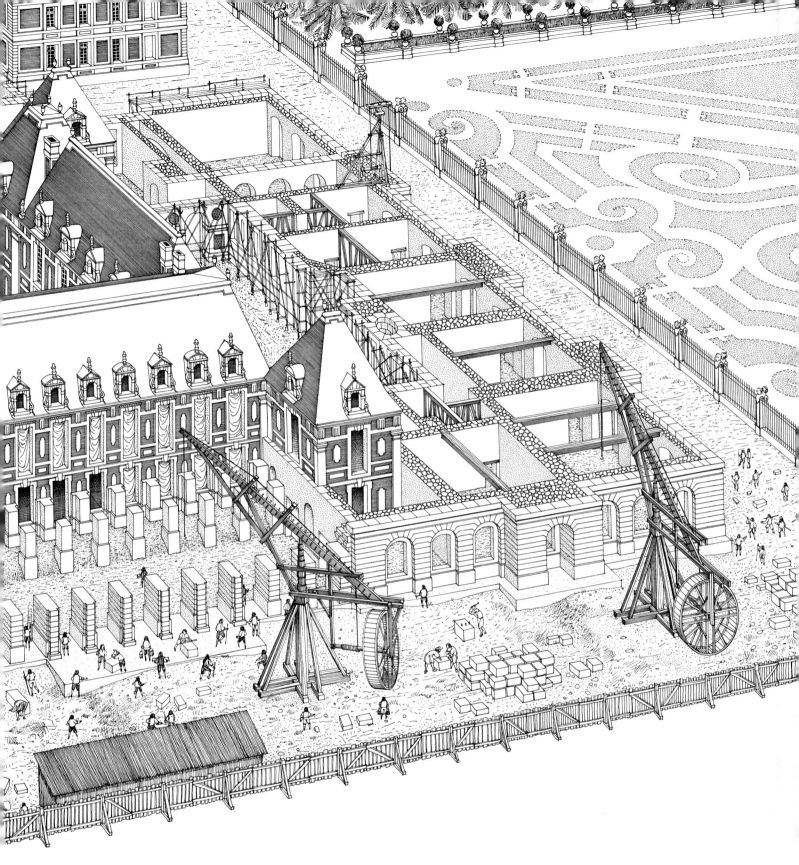

But, as the walls were going up, the King wondered whether he was right to refuse his architect's idea. Seeing his castle take shape, he feared that the old brick building, enclosed by the new buildings, would create a bad effect, when all was finished.

He hesitated for a few weeks, demanded a few modifications, and ended up proposing that the small castle should be demolished, but only if someone could propose a viable project to replace it, on the courtyard side.

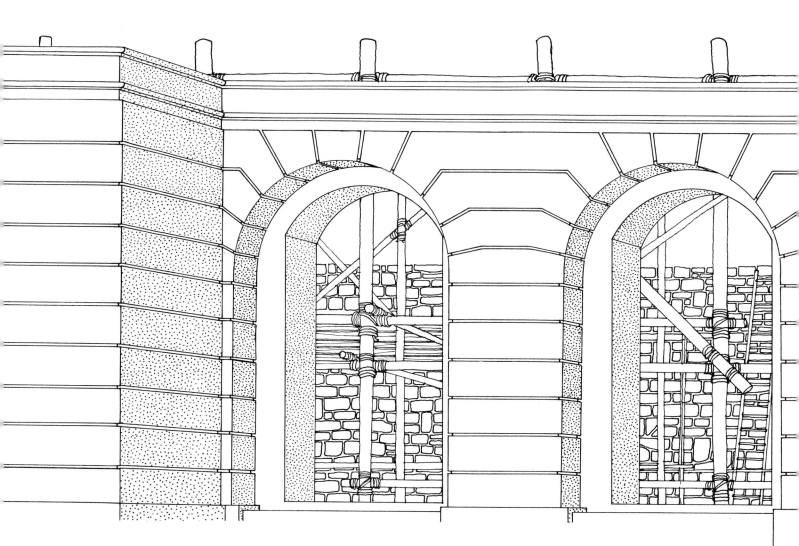

As this risked delaying the construction, they would have to act as soon as possible.

In the search for new ideas, the King was not content with demanding Le Vau's advice. He organized a competition open to all architects.

The competition was held at the end of June 1669. Six architects entered. Unfortunately, they were given insufficient time, so even by drawing night and day, they did not succeed in presenting a single acceptable project to replace the old castle.

The competition was cancelled. The King decided that as no one was capable of solving the problem, he would provisionally keep his old brick castle, until the far-off day when a talented architect could present a worthy project to replace it.

For Louis XIV, the affair was closed. But Le Vau was furious. He dared to attack again by trying this time, to convince the King that, in any case, the old castle was in bad shape and on the verge of collapsing. He pretended that it was essential to demolish it immediatly in order to prevent a catastrophe.

Clearly, the Architect's argument was so exaggerated that the King was offended. In an emotional voice, he replied that if someone wanted to demolish his small castle at all costs, he would not oppose it but he would have it rebuilt immediatly, without changing it in any way. Le Vau dared not insist any further.

In enlarging Versailles, Louis XIV had obtained a superb edifice but at the same time he had lost the intimacy of the small castle where, not so long ago, he had so enjoyed staying.

For this reason, he soon felt the need to build a new country house in the surrounding vicinity.

This country house was built in the park, one and a half kilometres away from the castle (the same distance from the Menagerie), on the site of an old village known as Trianon.

Gardens were landscaped and a series of small pavilions entitled *Trianon de Porcelaine** were erected.

The new residence was of freestone and its roofs were slate-covered. It seemed to be made of porcelain as it was blue and white, either real porcelain or earthenware from Holland or Normandy, or a painted imitation. It only took three months to build and it was ready at the same moment that the work at Versailles was completed, the beginning of the summer of 1670.

* Literal translation: Porcelain Trianon

47

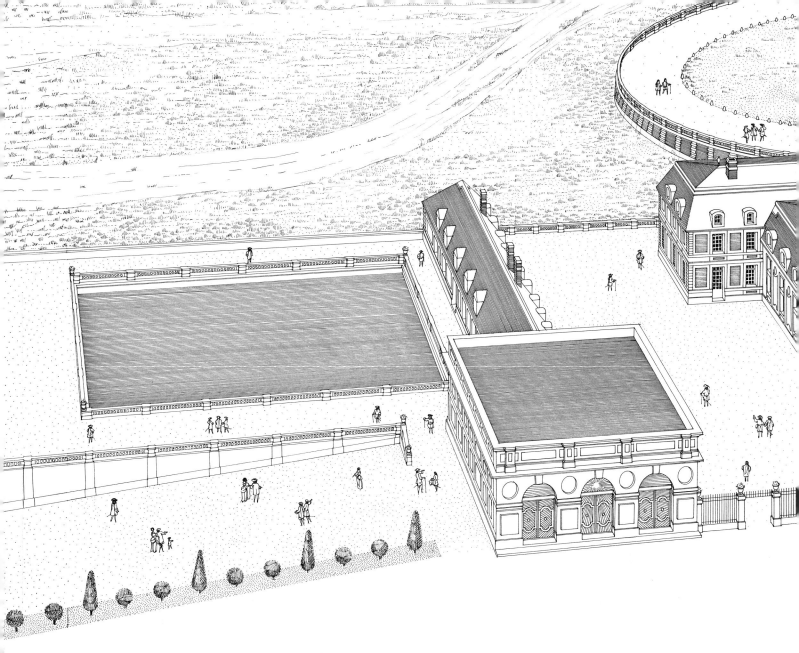

At Versailles, henceforth, the new castle encircled the old castle and completely hid it from the garden side.

In the middle of the main facade, a vast terrace cut it in half.
The left half was mainly for the King: Bathing Chamber on the ground floor, Grand Chamber on the first floor and Private Chamber above.
The right half was shared between the Queen, their children, the King's brother, his sister-in-law and his cousin.
But, the King and the Queen also kept their old chambers in the small castle.
Small amounts of space were found in various places to accommodate about ten extra people, but on the whole, the extension had only served to better accommodate those who had already had chambers in the old castle. Thus, Versailles still remained a private residence for the Royal Family, despite its extension and despite the construction of Trianon.

On the courtyard side, the castle had hardly changed as the new buildings disappeared behind the old building.

Only two small wings had been built, in the original style, in the
prolongation of the old castle, towards the kitchens on the right of the
court, and the stables on the left.

One could imagine that the work was finished. Nevertheless, before
the end of 1670, Louis XIV had already began new construction work.
He began with pavilions for the Ministers' accommodation, as the King
was obliged to have them nearby when he extended his visits to Versailles.

At roughly the same time, the new castle had to be lengthened in order
to join it to the kitchens and stables. A little bit later, these two buildings
were raised a floor. A lot more work was to follow...

From 1674 onwards, the castle and gardens of Versailles started to become famous throughout France and Europe.

It was known that Louis XIV was creating wonders, and this newly born reputation increasingly attracted curious visitors.

As the King now let everyone enter (the only condition was correct dress), visitors flooded in.

Guide books were published for them. In other words, the same type of small descriptive guide books we find today.

The first guide book appeared in 1674 and was writen by André Félibien. We will use it to visit the castle as it was he who showed the way...

He began by describing the avenues which led up to the castle, followed by the large square and successive courts which ended up here at the Marble Court.

This was the old court of Louis XIII's castle. It had just been paved in white, black and red marble, and enriched by a beautiful octagonal basin. The facades had not changed, they were now adorned with a collection of Roman busts placed on consoles. In the corners, fountains surmounted by gilded cast-iron bird cages were installed.

At the far end of the Court, a large gilded balcony was supported by eight red marble columns. Between the columns were three ironware doors, which were also gilded and led to the gardens.

Inside, nothing was finished and the first visitors at Versailles discovered a castle with little or no decor, with raw masonry and woodwork. The King's Grand Staircase was just an enormous empty volume.

Work was interrupted because of a lack of funds and because the King hesitated about the decoration and the layout of the steps. The giants who were to have held the cornice were later replaced by columns.

At the top of the staircase there was a living room entitled the *Grand Palier** followed by a hall opening onto the King's Grand Chamber.

This chamber consisted of six rooms.

The first one was naturally the Guardroom, followed by the Antechamber, the Bedroom and three *Cabinets***.

As they were installed on the first floor on the new buildings, all the rooms looked onto the gardens.

Behind, were the more intimate rooms: wardrobe, *Cabinet pour la chaise-percée*** and small private staircases.

Here we can see the King's Bedroom as it was in 1674. Its ceiling was decorated with large sculpted borders, designed to frame the paintings. These paintings were to have a link with the story of Antiquity and Louis XIV's symbol, Apollo.

But at this date, the paintings were not yet ready and the artists were working on them in their studios in Paris.

The walls, made of stone, rubble stone, plaster and wood, were to be hidden behind wooden wall panels which supported incredibly rich fabric, woven with silk, gold and silver threads.

These fabrics were also in the process of being manufactured.

Only the marble panels at the bottom of the walls, the cornice and the sculptures on the ceiling had been produced.

Even though his bedroom was unfinished, Louis XIV slept there every time he visited Versailles. He was satisfied with temporary furniture and tapestries which were removed as soon as he left.

A few years later, fabulous pieces of furniture in solid silver were delivered for the Bedroom and the other rooms in the Chamber. Unfortunately, Louis XIV was rapidly obliged to send them away to be melted down for coins.

* *Grand Landing*
** *Private rooms*
*** *Private room for the night commode (a seat with a hole, the ancestor of the toilet)*

After passing through the Grand Chamber, one arrived at the central terrace, which led to the Queen's Chamber.

This terrace, which dominated the gardens, stretched out level with the first floor, above the site of the old moat.

If we compare this view with those of pages 24 and 25, we can recognize the garden on the right and even certain windows on the left.

The terrace was paved in red, black and white marble with a white marble basin in the middle. A little later, this basin was ornamented by gilded bronze sculptures with fountains spouting out of them.

Sometimes, in the summer, orange trees were placed in pots on stone cubes along the edge, next to the garden.

The terrace did not last long. It was destroyed in 1678, because its pavings were not watertight and the leaking water was dangerous for the ground floor underneath. In its place, the Grand Gallery was built, which we will see later on.

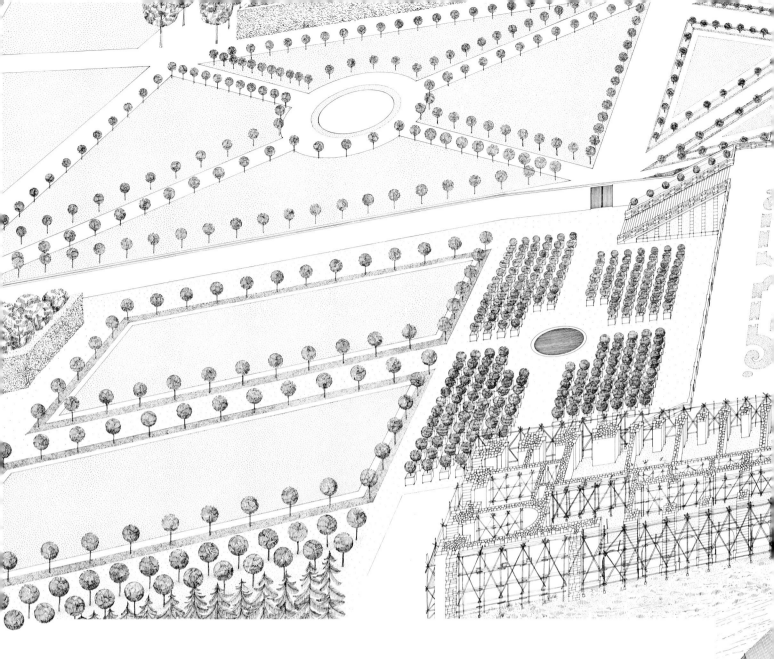

Around 1680, the castle had grown enormously and was still growing. An extra court had been traced in front of the castle. It was bordered by the *Ailes des Ministres**.

On the left, in the direction of the Orangery, a one hundred and fifty metre long building was being constructed. It was the *Aile du Midi***. A similar building was to be built opposite, on the right, on the site of the reservoirs. It was to be the *Aile du Nord****.

The village was slowly disappearing, invaded by the castle. Its old church, as well as Louis XIII's *jeu de paume* court were on the point of being replaced by new buildings.

Two years later, Versailles became the largest castle in Europe and Louis XIV made it his official residence. Several thousand courtiers and servants accompanied him, crowding themselves into the castle's innumerable quarters.

A new town sprang up around it to lodge all those with no accommodation in the Royal residence and for the tradesmen and trade necessary for the life of the Court.

* *The Ministers' Wings*
** *The South Wing*
*** *The North Wing*

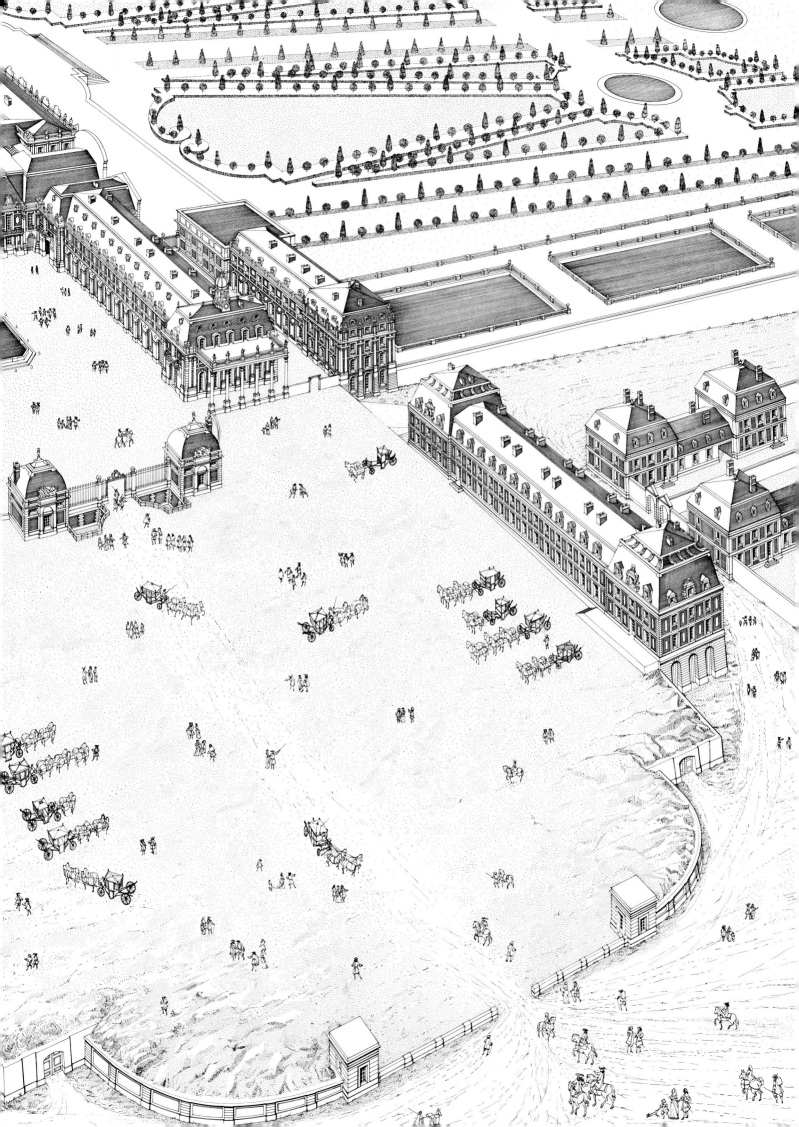

At this period, the inside of the château had a much more finished look. On the ground floor, one could visit the King's Bathing Chamber, whose main curiosity was the Cabinet which we can see here.

This room, entirely covered in multicolour marble, was divided into two sections which were separated by steps.

In the first section, there was an astonishing bath carved in a single block of red marble, in which several people could bathe together, while sitting on a bench in the water.

The bath was fed with either hot or cold water, according to choice, by pipes which came from a boiler and a reservoir which were behind the far wall. After usage, the water was drained by a sewer into a pond beyond the Orangery.

The second section of the room, raised by a flight of steps, was to be used for two individual baths, one on the right and one on the left. But they were never installed. When the marble masons delivered them, Louis XIV had just transformed the Cabinet by knocking down the steps and pushing the bath back.

The Grand Staircase had just been completed.

To render it even more majestic, an imposing perron with eleven red marble steps was added.

The pavings as well as the wall-covering were in white, red, green and black marble... Paintings and bronze gilded ornaments enhanced the overall effect.

In the middle of the arch was a glass ceiling which lit the staircase from above, a great novelty for the epoch.

This staircase was mostly used for Court ceremonies, such as receptions for Ambassadors.

Occasionally, the King held concerts. The orchestra was placed at the bottom of the staircase, whilst the landings and the steps were used as balconies and tiers for the spectators.

A lot later, at the time of Louis XV, even a theatre was installed. It was complemented by a stage and dismantable spectator boxes made of wood and painted canvas. This temporary theatre could hold eighty people: spectators, actors and musicians. But it had to be dismantled each time the staircase was needed for a ceremony.

Around 1684, the most spectacular transformation was undoubtedly the Grand Gallery. This immense room had just been built, on the first floor, on the site of the terrace.

It is often called the *Galerie des Glaces**, because of the seventeen mirrored arches which face the seventeen windows, which look onto the gardens.

When the decoration of the Grand Gallery was completed, Louis XIV reckoned that he had achieved his objectives.

After twenty years of work, he had succeeded in creating the largest and the most beautiful castle ever seen. This more than eradicated the affront of his Courtiers who had insulted him in the past when they had scorned his small house at Versailles.

Not only had he proved himself but his glory was assured.

He could finally return to his personal tastes which were steeped towards simplicity and nature.

In 1684, as he no longer wanted to play the ''Sun King'', he definitively abandoned his splendid Grand Chamber with its view of the garden and returned to live in the small castle of his childhood, which fortunately had been preserved, on the courtyard side.

He had a few transformations made to the interior so that he could install a chamber which catered to his real tastes. In other words, without marble or sculptures and ceilings without decorations. It was solely decorated with woodwork and white ceilings. Old Master paintings were his only luxury in this new chamber.

He had a *Cabinet du Billard** installed. The King greatly enjoyed this game. He mostly played with his son, his grandsons, his brother and his nephew, or with a few rare guests.

* *Billiard Room*

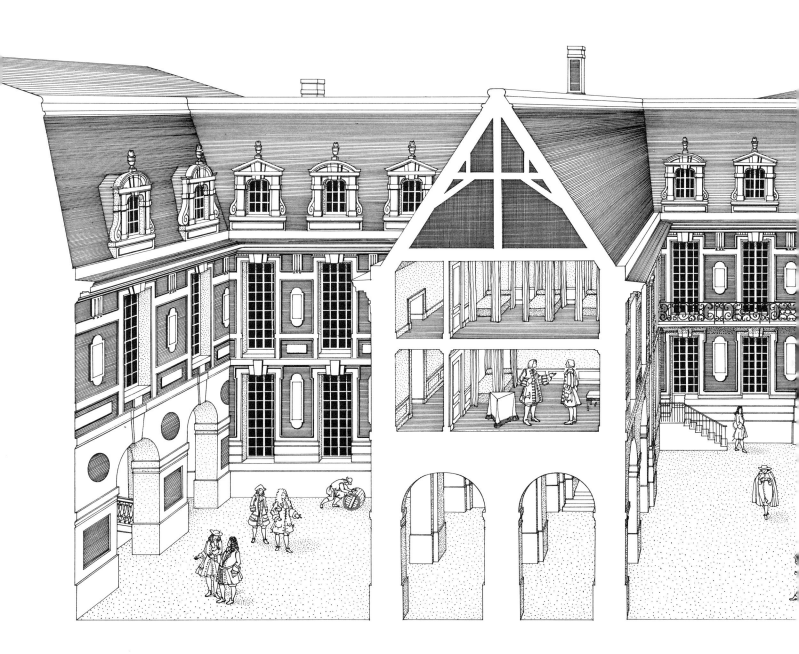

Thus, Louis XIV spent the last thirty-one years of his life on the courtyard side, steadfastly turning his back on the Grand Chambers which he had created for himself.

This drawing represents the interior courts: narrow, calm and almost secret, hidden behind the large official rooms.

The Grand Gallery is on the right. While in this room, one could not imagine the existence of these courts, even though they were so near. These were the King's courts. This was where Louis XIV had his personal rooms. Certain were very cramped and they took up several floors and mezzanines.

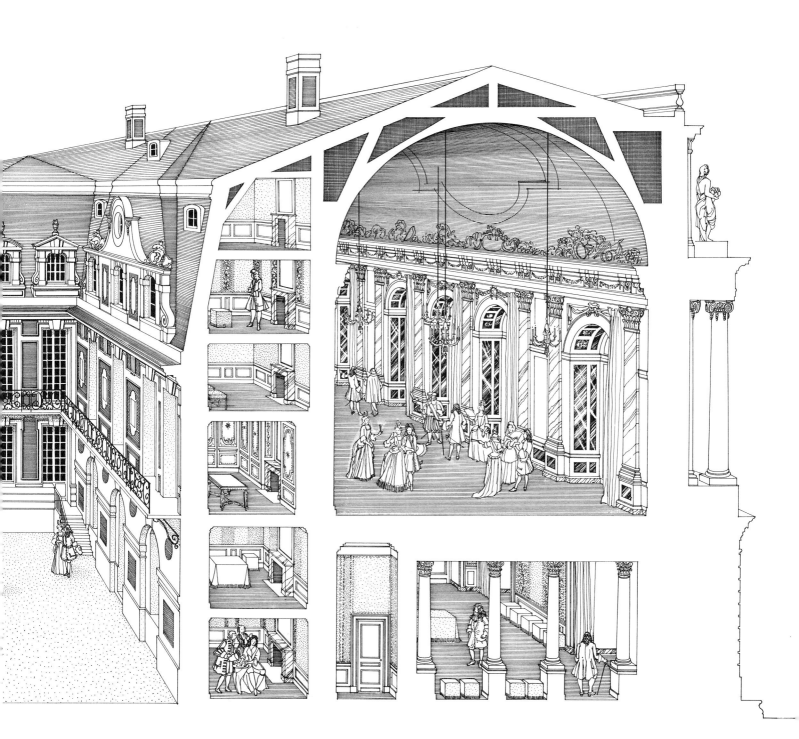

The first room, on the first floor to the left of the Gallery, was his small library. It opened, via two French windows, onto a balcony.

The next two French windows, just before the corner of the Court, gave onto a small staircase and the King's private Cabinet. The first two facing windows (still on the first floor) were those of the Cabinet where Louis XIV gathered his family every evening. The next two lit the *Cabinet du Billard*, which we saw on pages 72 and 73.

The building between the two courts contained the servants' bedrooms. Looking onto the other court, were the King's other Cabinets, which joined the Grand Staircase.

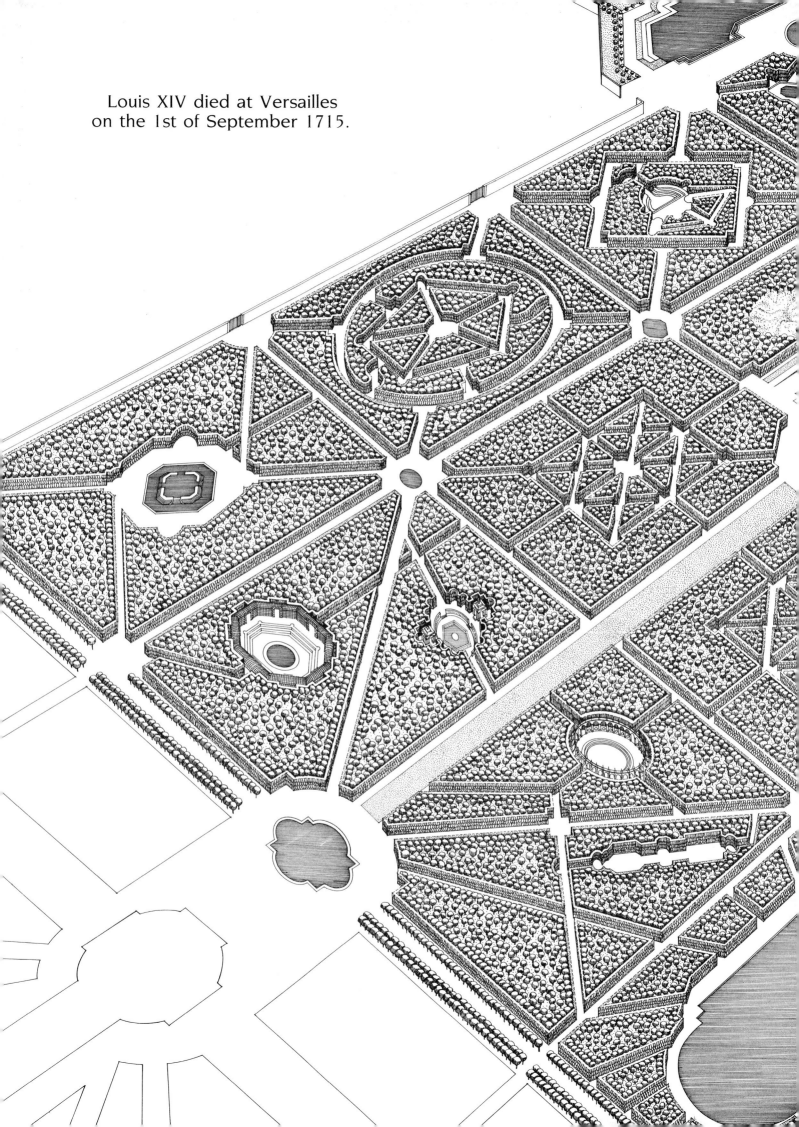

Louis XIV died at Versailles
on the 1st of September 1715.

Soon after, his great grandson, the young Louis XV left the château to live with the Court, first in Vincennes and then in Paris. During seven years, the estate remained abandoned, only receiving a few visitors from time to time.

Versailles was no doubt not only the most magnificient of all the royal castles, but the most impressive.

Louis XV, who was twelve years old when he returned to Versailles, was justifiably terrified at the thought of spending his whole life there.

A few rooms reserved for the King's education (library for studying and drawing, studio and laboratory for manual work...) were installed under the roofs. These were the only transformations made for a long time. Louis XV did not dare change anything, so intimidating was the memory of Louis XIV.

Then, bit by bit, as the years flowed by, Louis XIV was forgotten.
His official Grand Chambers would always be respected, but gradually his private Cabinets disappeared, to be replaced by new rooms, in which Louis XV ended up feeling at ease and at home.

Louis XV wanted to have a Bathing Chamber which was simpler and more comfortable than Louis XIV's.

He had it installed on the first floor, behind the Grand Chamber.

The installation was made up of several rooms: the Bathroom, as such, with two baths, one for the King and the other for a friend. This was because Louis XV, like Louis XIV, hated to bathe alone. This was in fact the fashion at the time; men often bathed in numbers, whilst women always bathed alone.

After leaving the Bathroom, one entered the Bedroom. The King relaxed on the bed after his bath. The friend who accompanied him had to be satisfied with an armchair or a stool.

Above, was the bedroom of the valets responsible for the upkeep of the Baths, as well as the premises where the boiler and the reservoir were installed. At this time, the reservoir was supplied by water carriers. Later on, a water pressure pump would be installed. Behind were the staircase and the reserve for toilet linen.

Under the roofs, Louis XV had a small private Chamber installed. He liked to come here to rest during his free time, alone or with a few intimate friends.

In fact, it was not really a chamber as it did not contain a bedroom. It was more like a suite of Cabinets. It included living rooms, a small gallery, several libraries and two dining rooms: one for the winter (which we can see here) and the other for summer, with a terrace of flowers.

All these rooms were adorned with carved woodwork, painted in lively and brilliant colours. The furniture, carpets and fabric created a perfectly refined whole and where also remarkably comfortable.

Above, by raising the old buildings from the time of Louis XIII and Louis XIV, several floors of kitchens were installed.

Unfortunately, in searching for comfort without respecting the architecture, Louis XV had ended up by giving the castle the same appearance as any other bourgeois city building.

This was further aggravated by the fact that everyone at Versailles wanted to imitate the King, and he let them do so. For example, the extraordinary small house with its railings, which can be seen on the ground floor on the court, was an idea of the King's daughters. They lived in this part of the château and the small house was their entrance. The railings stopped the public from coming right up underneath their windows.

On the left-hand side of the court, the roofs from Louis XIV's time (see pages 74 and 75) had been replaced by four floors of small chambers and kitchens. They could be reached by climbing the one hundred and thirty-six steps of the adjacent staircase.

The other staircase on the left was connected to the Courtier's chambers, above the Royal Grand Chamber.

All this was no longer a real castle, but a type of labyrinth in which one could easily get lost. Even more so as the staircases and corridors were perpetually transformed or moved.

Obviously, these muddled transformations had upset a lot of people.

More than anybody, Ange-Jacques Gabriel, the King's First Architect, was appalled. He thought that, rather than continuing to pile up the small rooms, the King would be better off giving Versailles the appearance of royal majesty which it had always lacked.

He knew that Louis XIV's First Architect had dreamt of demolishing Louis XIII's old brick and slate castle.

Like his faraway predecessor, Gabriel wished to replace these old buildings, on the courtyard side, with large white stone buildings similar to those which Louis XIV had previously built on the garden side.

Thus, the whole château would have been built in the same style and would have become worthy of its royal function.

For thirty years, he persisted in trying to convince the King.

For thirty years, Louis XV refused. Finally, in 1771, weary of so much insistence, he ended up by accepting. To convince the King, Gabriel had employed the same trick as Le Vau. He used the poor condition of the old castle as a pretext.

Reconstruction work on the courtyard side began by replacing the old brick wing on the right by a new stone wing.

But Louis XV did not have the time to finish the work he undertook. He died on the 10th of May 1774. The building on the right remained uncompleted, and most of the old remaining brick facades were intact.

The new King, Louis XVI, could not continue Louis XV his grandfather's work. Funds were lacking and during the fifteen years which he stayed at Versailles, he only had the opportunity to make a few interior transformations.

The epoch of the grand construction work was well and truly over.

In 1789, the French Revolution erupted, and on the 6th of October, a crowd of rioting Parisians descended onto Versailles to force the King, the Queen, the Royal Family and the Court to leave the château.

The French monarchy no longer existed. Versailles, the castle of the last four Kings, had no further use.

There were people who thought that the best thing to do would be to demolish it, destroy the gardens and hand the land over to agriculture.

Fortunately, no one listened to them and the château was saved. Nothing was destroyed, the revolutionaries were content with effacing all the royal emblems, such as crowns, *fleur-de-lis**, etc.

They also removed all the furniture, wall coverings and objects of art. Nearly everything was sold by auction.

Thus, Versailles furniture was scattered throughout the world, in Europe and America.

* *Royal arms of France*

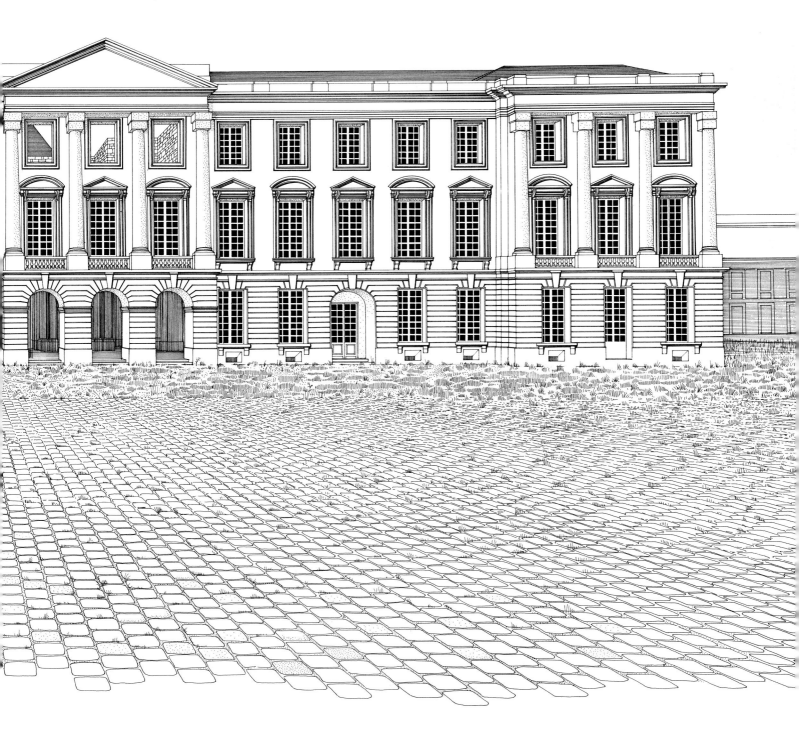

Versailles, unlived and empty, had become a desert. Several projects were proposed: a museum, a school and a hospital. But none of these propositions had much success and nothing succeeded in reviving the château.

Slowly, it deteriorated. In several places, rain dripped through the roofing. In the courts, grass growed between the pavings, large blocks of facade threatened to collapse, and had Napoleon not made some urgent repairs, the château would have fallen into ruin and disappeared for good.

After 1814, King Louis XVIII put onto the throne of his ancestors, wished to reinstate himself at Versailles. He began a general restoration of the château, but in the end, he never returned to live there.

In 1883, King Louis-Philippe found a definitive use by turning it into a museum of the History of France. In other words, a museum with thousands of paintings and statues representing important events and famous men throughout the History of France.

Obviously such a museum demanded large rooms which were easily accessible to the public, with naked walls to hang paintings. To obtain such rooms, it was necessary to demolish a lot of the old rooms.

The Royal Chambers were respected, but those of the Princes and Courtiers were destroyed. It needed four years to tear out the woodwork and the chimneys, demolish partitions, floors and staircases.

Thus, the "1830 Room" hereby represented, was created on the site of more than thirty old rooms irreversibly destroyed.

Today, as in the past, the château of Versailles welcomes the public. What the visitors discover in going through the gates and entering the courts, is of course Louis XIV's castle. But it is also three centuries of work during which Versailles was formed then transformed.

The first court dates back to 1670, but the two long wings which surround it were not built until 1678.

The second court, which opens with a statue of Louis XIV (1837), is closed on the right by a wing with columns and frontons (1771) in which the large staircase (only recently built in 1986) is situated, and on the left by a pavilion (1815), extended by the old stables (1662). Behind, two short wings (1670) finally rejoin the old castle of Louis XIII (1631-1634).

This mixture of epochs and styles can seem odd, but it gives the château a fantasy and off-hand air which make all its charm.

However, it is this fantasy which has always been critized by the serious-minded, since the very beginning of the château's existence. A lot of people would have preferred impeccable architecture, respecting a unity of style and the rules of art. If Louis XIV and his successors had listened to them, Versailles would have been perfect, majestic but sinister.

Let us, however, leave the last words to the serious-minded by offering Colbert the last page. This would be the perfect occasion to conclude by giving a friendly, but respectful wink to Louis XIV.

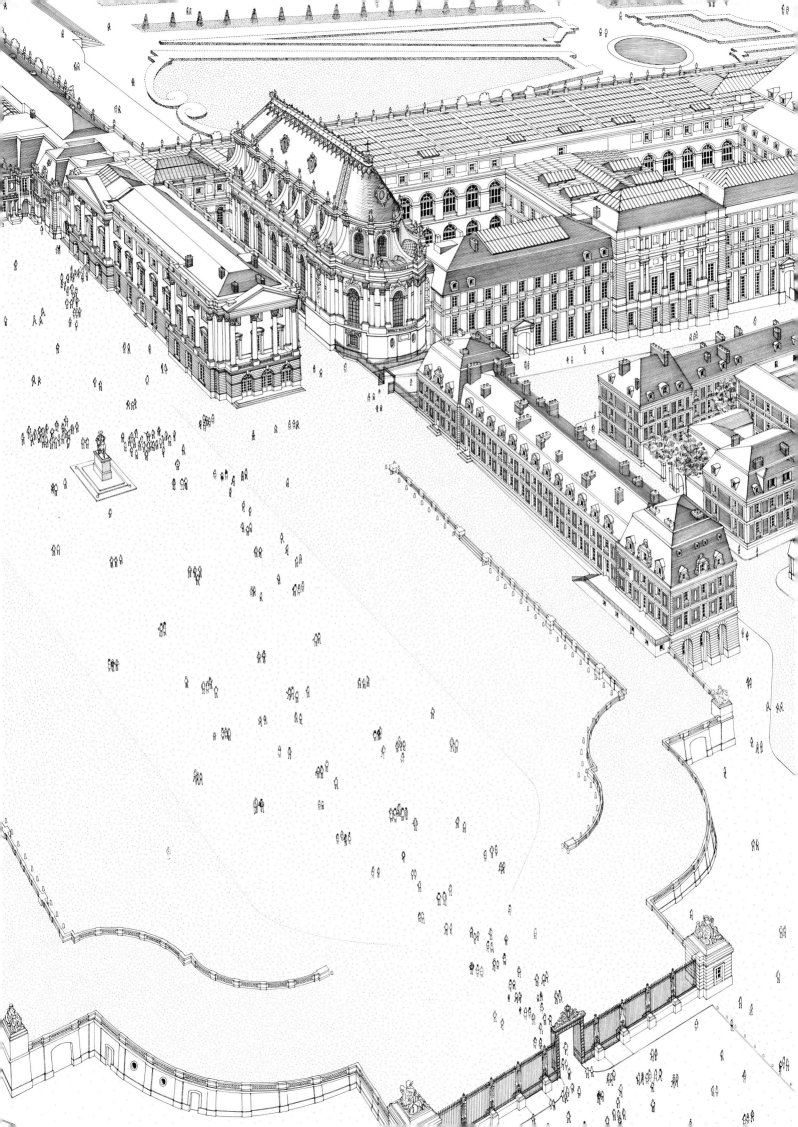

All men who have taste in architecture,
and in the present and in the future,
will find that this castle resembles a small man
with long arms, a large head,
in other words A MONSTER OF BUILDINGS.

JEAN-BAPTISTE COLBERT

Minister and Secretary of State
General Controller of Finances
Superintendent of the King's Buildings

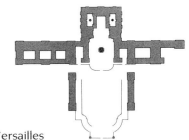

Plan of the château of Versailles

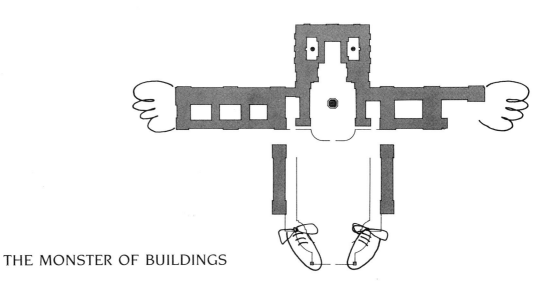

THE MONSTER OF BUILDINGS

VERSAILLES LOCATIONS

All the locations of the château presented in this book have been studied with the minutest care. Certain still exist, but a lot of them have disappeared. On this page, we list those that have replaced them. Other locations have evolved progressively as we have seen all along this book.

EXISTING LOCATIONS

LOCATIONS WHICH HAVE DISAPPEARED

* *Games Cabinet of Madame du Barry*
** *Literal translation: The Antechamber of the Bull's Eye (small circular window)*
*** *Court of the Grand Common*
**** *Museum of the Grand Stable*
***** *Marble Trianon*

Loi n° 49-956 du 16 juillet 1949 sur les publications destinées à la Jeunesse
Dépôt légal mars 1990 - Deux Coqs d'Or éditeur - N° 1/3-9307 - 11-89
Imprimé en Italie (49)